Me, Hemorrhage

Me, Hemorrhage

Recovery from a Ruptured Arteriovenous Malformation

Carol Hollar-Zwick

ISBN-13: 9798551261766

For Christopher and Brayden

Foreword

I met Chris Rajchel a few years ago at a Hardee's in Appleton, Wisconsin. Chris suggested meeting there after his mother contacted me through the English department where I was teaching. She had explained that Chris was disabled and was looking for a writer to help him tell his life story. I was intrigued.

"Me, Packer hat," Chris said when I called to confirm our first meeting.

"I'm wearing a red scarf," I said.

"Hardee's. See you," he said and hung up.

When I got in my car and mapped my destination, I realized that there was more than one Hardee's in Appleton, and I didn't know which one Chris was headed to. I called him back, but he couldn't tell me where to go because he wasn't able to explain exactly where he was. I was late to our first meeting, but I found him. We recognized each other immediately: He was wearing a Green Bay Packers hat, and I was wearing a red scarf.

"Good to see you, good to see you," Chris said, smiling and holding out his left hand for me to shake.

Over the next hour, Chris made clear that he wanted to write a book about his life, but it became evident that he would need more help than I had expected. He had suffered a brain hemorrhage ten years earlier that left permanent damage. He was no longer able to read or express himself fully in words. Still, he had a plan for the two of us to interview his family and friends. Together, we would piece together his life before and after the hemorrhage.

Expressing his wishes wasn't easy for him that day, nor were they easy for me to interpret. There was a lot of back and forth, and gradually I understood what he had in mind. I asked a lot of questions, and I learned to adapt my questioning to the kinds of answers Chris could provide. It was like a very complex game of twenty questions. Chris wrote dates and numbers on paper to help me grasp key pieces of information. I decided to think about it, and I told him I'd get back to him. Ultimately, I said I'd give it a try.

Over the next year, through laughter and tears, Chris and I interviewed his mother, Candace Ascher; his mother-in-law, Myra Harris; his brother, Rick Rajchel; and his friends Rich Olson, Sean McPeak, Lisa McPeak, and Shawn Murphy (Murf). Chris drove me around his childhood home, and I spent time with his delightful sons, Christopher and Brayden. Through these people and experiences, I learned about other important people in Chris's life who shaped him as a young person and who supported him since the hemorrhage: his ex-wife, Holly Rajchel; his stepfather, Mike Ascher, who died in 2016 after 28 years of marriage to Chris's mother; and Chris's close friend Todd Duellman, who died tragically with his father in a highway accident in 2001. Chris has a tattoo in remembrance of Todd, and he remains close to Todd's sister, Terri, and his family.

I also pored over Chris's medical records from 2007 through 2014, which Chris provided. The records were invaluable in blending the emotional memories of his friends and family with the hard facts recorded by his doctors and therapists. With that information and additional research, I have assembled a narrative of Chris's life before, during, and after the hemorrhage.

Imagine for a moment that you have a thought you want to say, but the words just won't come. You try and try, but you cannot say the words you want to say. Or imagine you are trying to speak a language you don't know very well. You have a limited number of ways to express an idea. If the person you're talking to doesn't understand, you can't simply explain your thought another way. You keep trying, but if the person you're talking to isn't trying to understand you, the communication won't be successful. Chris lives through this every day.

Chris's story is one of perseverance. He was lucky to survive the brain hemorrhage, but he was unlucky to be left with brain damage that limited his capacity with language. And yet he does communicate: He has strong relationships with friends and family, and especially with his two sons. He has tremendous drive to be fully in this life.

Bleed

On March 9, 2007, the left side of Chris Rajchel's brain began to bleed. He was 34 years old, married, and the father of two preschool-aged boys.

Chris was in the shower when the bleeding started. First he had a hot flash and a sudden headache. Then he began gasping for breath. He got out of the shower and sat in a rocking chair in his living room, trying to breathe. His language became confused and incoherent gibberish. The pupil of his left eye dilated as he had a seizure and lost consciousness.

Chris's wife, Holly, called 911 and screamed as loud as she could for Rich, Chris's best friend from childhood who lived on the second floor of the duplex he owned with Chris and Holly. Rich raced downstairs, and together he and Holly carried Chris to the bedroom. They placed him on the bed and dressed him while they waited for the ambulance.

Holly suspected right away that Chris's brain was hemorrhaging. Two months earlier, Chris had been diagnosed with an arteriovenous malformation (AVM) in the left hemisphere of his brain. An AVM is a tangle of abnormal blood vessels connecting arteries and veins. The vessels fold into one another and grow into a ball. In Chris's brain, the AVM had grown enough for him to begin experiencing numbness and tingling that led to his diagnosis.

The numbness and tingling had started in August of 2006. Chris was at work at TDS Metrocom when the thumb, index finger, and third finger of his right hand went a little numb. It happened again a month or so later. Then he had a spell of numbness and tingling in his right cheek and lip. It didn't seem serious, and he had no other symptoms: His arm felt normal, his vision and hearing were normal, and he had no weakness or dizziness.

After several months, the tingling and numbness were occurring frequently enough that he told Holly, who urged him to see his primary care physician. His doctor referred him to specialists, who began a battery of tests. Chris had a brain MRI at the end of December. Shortly after the MRI, he underwent cerebral angiography, also known as a brain angiogram, a procedure that uses a catheter, contrast fluid, and x-ray imaging to examine the blood vessels in the brain for abnormalities. In early January, Chris was told he had an AVM.

Three days before Chris's brain began bleeding, he had undergone the second of five planned embolization procedures aimed to cut off the blood supply to the AVM.

When the paramedics arrived, Chris was in a semi-comatose state and in acute distress. His left pupil was dilated, and he was decerebrate, a term that describes a patient whose muscles are tight and rigid, causing the head and neck to arch and holding the toes, arms, and legs out straight. Being decerebrate was also a sign that severe damage was happening to Chris's brain, which the paramedics recognized. Chris was also struggling to breathe, and the paramedics gave him oxygen as the ambulance raced to the hospital.

In the emergency room, the doctors intubated Chris and tried to stabilize him as his brain continued to bleed. They ordered a CT scan, which showed a hematoma—a mass of blood—about three inches in diameter in his brain, just below the area of the AVM that had been embolized three days before.

Chris was comatose and near death as the ER doctors prepped him for emergency surgery. Holly was brought to his bedside in case he didn't make it through. Then he was whisked away to the operating room for surgery that took eight hours.

Holly and Rich followed the ambulance in Rich's car. According to Rich, Chris died three times on the way to Theda Clark Hospital in Neenah, where Chris's doctors practiced.

Holly began making calls as they drove. She was nearly hysterical when she reached her mother, Myra, who had just put the couple's young sons, Christopher and Brayden, down for afternoon naps. Then she called Chris's brother, Rick, and asked him to call their mother, Candace. When Candace got Rick's call, she threw things in a bag and began the four-and-a-half-hour drive from Siren, Wisconsin, with her husband, Mike. Holly then called Sean and Lisa, whom she and Chris had planned to spend the evening with, and Chris's friend Murf. "It's really bad," she said. "It's about as bad as it gets."

Friends called other friends and co-workers, and a small, subdued crowd gathered at the hospital to wait and worry with Holly, Rich, and Rick as the surgeons did what they could to save Chris's life. At one point a hospital chaplain approached Rick, and he panicked, thinking the chaplain had come to tell Holly that Chris had died. Thankfully he had come to offer support while Chris was still in surgery.

"It was the worst day of my life," Rich said, thinking back to that day. "Chris was like a brother to me. At one point, the doctors gave him a 15 percent chance of survival."

Things did not go as well in the operating room as Chris's surgeon would have liked.

The surgeon first performed a decompressive craniectomy to remove a piece of Chris's skull and create more space for his brain, which was swelling due to the growing hematoma. Opening up Chris's skull would relieve the pressure on his brain and protect it from further damage. The surgeon made a large incision in Chris's scalp and used a drill to cut through the bone. A piece of bone was removed, cleaned, and placed in a sterile container for storage until it could be replaced. That part went well

The bigger challenge was locating the hematoma, which was difficult because it was on the underside of Chris's brain. The surgeon first attempted to locate it using ultrasound, but the ultrasound machine didn't work properly. He then decided to perform a corticectomy to locate the hematoma, a procedure in which a specific portion of the cerebral cortex is removed. Yet despite being careful to avoid the nidus, or base, of the AVM, a small tuft of blood vessels from the nidus ruptured and added to the bleeding. The surgeon attempted to cauterize these blood vessels, but he was successful only in slowing the bleeding. The left side of Chris's brain swelled even more as the AVM continued to hemorrhage.

At that point, the surgeon had done all he could to stop the bleeding. He placed sterile cotton balls in the hematoma to absorb the blood, drilled a hole in Chris's skull to relieve the swelling and pressure on his brain, and placed a monitor inside his skull to measure the pressure. The surgical team cleaned and covered the wounds, and Chris was moved to the intensive care unit. The pressure in Chris's skull remained high after surgery—around 30 mmHg—compared to a normal level of 7-15 mmHg. Chris was given a blood transfusion and placed in an induced coma to allow his brain to rest and begin to recover.

Later that evening, the pressure in Chris's brain grew dangerously high. He was brought back to the operating room, where the surgeon inserted a second, external drain. The procedure was successful in alleviating the pressure on Chris's brain, and he again was placed in an induced coma.

The surgeon's notes from that day describe Chris's situation as dire and his prognosis as uncertain. When he talked to Holly after the surgery, he told her that on a scale from one to 10, Chris was a 9.5. Later, after Chris had recovered, the surgeon told Holly that he'd had three similar cases in his career, and all the patients had died. Chris was the first to survive.

Diagnosis

Arteriovenous malformations are very rare and affect less than one percent of the population. When they occur, they most commonly appear in the brain or the spine, and for reasons that are not well understood, they occur more commonly in men than women. Like most AVMs, Chris's AVM probably developed when his mother was pregnant with him. He didn't have symptoms until his thirties, which is often the case. Some people never have symptoms.

AVMs are analyzed and rated using the Spetzler-Martin scale, which takes into account the size, drainage, and location of an AVM. The AVM in Chris's brain was rated a grade 4 (out of 6) on the Spetzler-Martin. At 4.5 centimeters, Chris's AVM was quite large. The venous drainage of the AVM was both superficial and deep. It was located in an area of eloquent cortex of Chris's brain, specifically in the parietal lobe of the left hemisphere of his brain, a region at the top of his head, roughly in the middle and behind the frontal lobe and in front of the occipital lobe.

The location of the AVM in an area of eloquent cortex was a stroke of bad luck for Chris. Eloquent cortex areas of the brain control sensory processing, linguistic ability, and large motor control. Damage to these areas of the brain can result in paralysis as well as losses in sensory processing, language comprehension and speech, including reading and writing. For Chris, the extent of the damage to his brain could only be determined by what he was able to do—and not able to do—as he recovered.

The biggest danger of having an AVM is rupture, bleeding, and the potential for damage to the brain as a result. An AVM puts extreme pressure on the walls of the affected arteries and veins. Over time, the pressure can thin and weaken the walls and increase the risk of hemorrhage. Treatment is often proposed to reduce these risks.

The size, drainage, and location of the AVM in Chris's brain ruled out surgery as a treatment option. Instead, Chris's doctors proposed a series of five embolization procedures to block the flow of blood to the AVM, followed by stereotactic radiosurgery, known more commonly as CyberKnife. The embolization procedures would involve running a catheter from an artery in Chris's leg to his brain and filling the blood vessels with a synthetic, glue-like substance near the AVM to block off the blood flow to it. The embolization procedures were to be followed by CyberKnife procedures, which would use radiation to damage the veins and arteries in the AVM to the point that they would shrink to nothing. At the time Chris was diagnosed, CyberKnife was not available at the hospital where he was being treated, though plans were in the works for the surgeons there to start using the procedure several months after Chris began embolization treatments.

Treatment

"This is uncharted territory," Holly said to her mother when Chris was diagnosed. "I'd rather you have the boys so I can take care of whatever happens."

Christopher and Brayden were three and one years old when the embolization procedures started in February 2007. Holly and Chris didn't know how he would respond to the treatment, but both knew that there was a 15 percent risk of hemorrhage after each procedure. Holly needed to be available in case there were complications, so Myra flew to Wisconsin in February, picked up the two little boys and their things, and flew back with them to her home in Alabama. She had started taking the boys to spend a month with her in the summer when Christopher was a year old, and the boys had stayed with her between Thanksgiving and Christmas, so she was accustomed to caring for her grandsons. She welcomed the opportunity to help.

The first embolization procedure, on February 19, went smoothly. After the procedure, however, and while Chris was in the hospital, he experienced a spike in seizure activity, which his doctors feared might be a hemorrhage associated with the procedure. He had numbness in his right hand, which he'd had before, and slurred speech, which was new. He admitted that the week before the embolization procedure he had stopped taking Keppra, an anti-seizure medication he was prescribed in January, because it caused insomnia and lethargy. His doctors resumed Keppra immediately at a high, "loading" dose level via his IV. Happily, a CT scan of Chris's brain showed no bleeding, and he was released the next day with instructions to continue taking Keppra, to start taking aspirin as a blood thinner, and to avoid heavy lifting, strenuous exercise, stressful emotional situations, alcohol, and smoking.

The second embolization took place on March 6, and it also went smoothly. Chris had some numbness in his right thumb and forefinger afterward, but upon discharge only the tip of his right thumb was numb. At that point, the AVM was diagnosed as partially embolized. The next embolization was scheduled for March 21.

Disaster struck three days later. It was March 9, Holly's birthday, and she had taken the day off from work to spend time with Chris and their good friends, Sean and Lisa, who were engaged. They had asked Chris and Holly to stand up at the wedding they were planning in Mexico.

Chris's doctors had stressed that Chris should not drink, so instead of going out to celebrate Holly's birthday, the two couples planned to spend the evening at Holly and Chris's home. That morning, Lisa had put crockpots of food she'd made in her car, which would stay cold in the early March temperatures while she was at work. She was devastated when she got Rich's call. She called Sean, and the two rushed to the hospital. They became part of a group sitting with Holly, tensely awaiting news about Chris's condition from the medical team.

Holly

Although Chris had many girlfriends in his teens and twenties, Holly was different. Chris made that clear to his mother when he introduced Holly to Candace at the funeral for his close friend Todd, who had died in a car accident. Holly was a special person in Chris's life.

Chris had met Holly at Fraser's, a neighborhood bar that was the center of his social life. Chris had worked there as a bartender for a while, and he had met several of his friends there, including Sean and Murf.

Holly came in one night with Lisa and other friends from work. Chris and Sean were talking, and Chris caught Holly's eye. Sean knew Holly from work, and he introduced them. The chemistry was instant. They talked all that evening, and they began seeing each other regularly.

Chris was completely smitten. He saw Holly as much as he could, staying up all night talking with her. Murf was Chris's roommate at the time, and he hardly saw him: Chris worked, went out, and spent time with Holly.

"Life of the party."
"Charismatic to the extreme."

"Larger than life."

"Walk-in-the-room, take-over-the-place kind of guy."

Those are just a few of the ways Chris's friends described him. Charming and good-looking, he had a way of drawing people to him, and he always had people around him. According to Murf, Chris was happiest and most comfortable being the center of attention; he was "the guy all the girls wanted to be with, and all the guys wanted to be."

Dark-haired, pretty, and vivacious, Holly was similarly outgoing and charismatic. She had a strong personality, and in Chris she found someone whose personality was even stronger than hers. She found his confidence attractive, Lisa observed. They dated for a year and were married in 2002.

A late spring snow fell on April 6, the night of Chris and Holly's wedding. Chris's stepdad, Mike, a United Methodist pastor, performed the ceremony, and Rich served as Chris's best man. Afterward, Chris and Holly's many friends and relatives from Wisconsin (Chris's side) and the South (Holly's side) danced to a DJ.

Myra, Sean, and Lisa helped with the wedding. The day before, Myra and several friends prepared the food for the rehearsal dinner, which Sean and Lisa hosted in the basement of Sean's house. On the wedding day, Myra decorated the venue, a big house, with wedding decorations she had mailed to Wisconsin the week before.

Newly married, Chris and Holly moved from an apartment to 1920s Victorian duplex they bought with Rich near downtown Appleton. They were fun-loving and outgoing, seeing friends on weeknights, having campfires in the summer, and going on snowmobiling trips in the winter.

They wanted children, and in June 2003 Christopher was born. Myra and Candace were there, waiting together while Chris supported Holly. Two years later, in March 2005, Brayden was born.

Holly and Chris doted on the boys. Both were attentive parents, taking turns feeding, diapering, dressing, and comforting their sons. "Chris was a wonderful dad," Myra said, "a hands-on dad."

ICU

Chris spent four hard weeks in the intensive care unit recovering from the brain hemorrhage and suffering from many complications:

He developed deep-vein thrombosis—blood clots—in both his arms and in his left leg. An inferior vena cava filter, a device to prevent blood clots from traveling through the blood to his lungs, was surgically placed on March 19.

The external drain that was placed in his skull during the night of March 9 stopped working—Chris had developed "shunt dependency"—and was replaced by a new shunt on March 28. The new shunt routed the fluid building up in his brain to his gut and kept the pressure in his brain at an acceptable level.

He developed ventilator-associated pneumonia that required antibiotics.

On April 4, doctors performed a tracheostomy, placing a breathing tube inserted in his throat. During the same surgery on April 4, a feeding tube was inserted into his stomach.

He was weaned off the ventilator, but he was placed back on it because he began to gag and cough.

Despite the complications, Chris began to recover.

Holly brought pictures of Christopher and Brayden and taped them to the wall where Chris could see them when he was brought out of the coma.

"I don't want them to look at Chris as a statistic, or a just a patient," she told her mother on the phone, who still had Christopher and Brayden with her in Alabama. "I want them to know that he's got these boys, and that they do all they can to get him back to the boys."

Holly was at Chris's bedside nearly round the clock, talking to him and rubbing lotion on his feet and hands to fight the dryness that was setting in. Already a petite woman, she lost weight she couldn't afford to lose. Holly's friends rallied to her side, communicating among themselves how best to care for her while she cared for Chris. They brought food to her at the hospital, took shifts sitting with her in the ICU, and sent her home to sleep. Life became a blur of the hospital and sleep.

Candace made the drive from Siren about every two weeks, staying for a few days each time. Rick was at the hospital daily. Myra's community supported Chris and Holly from afar. Her church in Mississippi, where Myra had lived for 41 years, raised over $700 to offset Chris and Holly's expenses.

On March 23, two weeks into those four hard weeks, the swelling in Chris's brain had gone down enough that his medical team decided it was safe to bring Chris out of the induced coma. They brought him out slowly, monitoring his brain activity at each step.

Chris could recognize Holly and Rich pretty much immediately, but he couldn't recognize everyone he saw. He could hear and respond to questions by moving his head to indicate *yes* and *no*, but he could not speak. He was unable to move his right arm and leg.

Chris was breathing on his own by the end of March. The process of figuring out the extent of the damage to his brain began.

Chris

Until the hemorrhage, Chris had lived a fairly ordinary life by American standards. He was born in Milwaukee in 1972, two years after his brother Rick. His father, Ron, was in the Navy, and he and Candace had moved from Wisconsin to Illinois and then to Rhode Island when the boys were young.

Ron and Candace divorced when Rick and Chris were five and three years old, respectively. At that point, Ron moved to Massachusetts and out of his sons' lives. Rick and Chris heard from him so infrequently that they eventually began referring to him as "Sperm Donor." Even though Ron told Rick he would visit Chris after the hemorrhage, he never came.

After a few years as a single mom, Candace married Jim Schultz and moved with Rick and Chris to Underhill, Wisconsin, a rural community of about 850 people in the northeastern part of the state. They lived in the town's tiny downtown, which had a handful of tidy houses, a general store, a park, a post office, and a couple of bars. The boys attended school in Gillett, a nearby town of about 1500 people, where Candace's mother had gone to high school.

Candace's parents had moved to Underhill several years before, and Chris and Rick loved spending time with their grandparents. They visited their grandpa every Saturday and spent summer days exploring their grandparents' property and pounding buckets of nails into stumps in the front yard. Their new stepdad wasn't much of a father figure. A carpenter by trade, he put the boys to work during their school breaks. One summer he had them pull nails out of stacks of boards, a task much less fun than pounding nails into stumps with their grandfather. Together, Chris and Rick filled a 55-gallon drum with nails.

Chris loved living in Underhill. The family lived across the street from the town park located in one corner of the downtown, an expanse of green grass with a playground and a baseball field that sloped to the Oconto River. The kids in town played tag in the summer and went sledding in the winter. Chris and Rick tucked themselves into garbage cans and rolled each other down the hill toward the river. One summer Chris served as the local baseball team's unofficial water boy. When he was old enough, he biked the country roads to his grandparents' house and to friends' houses.

He met Rich, who was four years older and became his best and lifelong friend. Chris and Rich rode bikes together when they were young and later built minibikes that they raced on the dairy farm where Rich grew up. They converted an old chicken coop on the farm to "The Shack," where they spent time hanging out with friends, playing cards, smoking, watching TV, listening to heavy metal, drinking Mountain Dew, and later, beer when they could get their hands on it. Rich claimed he corrupted Chris by giving him his first cigarette when he was 10 and his first beer when he was 14, but Chris's uncles had beaten him to the punch by getting Chris and Rick drunk on Mountain Dew and whiskey when they were 12 and 14.

Candace divorced Jim when Chris was 13. Two years later, she married Mike Ascher, her co-star in "Murder at the Howard Johnson's" at a theater in Shawano, and moved with the boys to Bonduel, a town about 15 miles south of Underhill. Candace and Mike blended their families in a yellow two-story house they had built on a corner—Chris, Rick, Karl, Eric, and Sarah--five teenagers ranging in age from 15 to 19. There was a big empty lot next door, and neighbor kids poured out of their houses during halftime of Packer games to play football.

Chris started his sophomore year at Bonduel High School. He joined the football team, but his season ended prematurely—and abruptly—when his stepbrother Karl, a year older than Chris, tackled him during practice and broke his collarbone.

Chris enjoyed the social aspects of high school more than the academic side. Tall and handsome, with a winning smile and gray-blue eyes, he was fun-loving and rowdy, and he loved to talk and party. When Chris was old enough to drive, he cruised from town to town on weekend nights with Rich and his new friend Todd, more than once landing in a ditch. He failed English as a senior, but Candace made sure he graduated by driving him to a nearby town for a remedial class. He was smarter than his grades indicated, and he graduated with his class in 1990.

Chris enlisted in the Air Force three months after graduation, following in the footsteps of his father, uncles, and grandfather. He was stationed at Nellis Air Base in Las Vegas, where he trained as a truck mechanic. He deployed to Saudi Arabia for a year in the aftermath of Operation Desert Storm. Back in Las Vegas, he married a woman who left him after three months without filing for divorce. When Chris and Holly got engaged, he had to track her down to sign the divorce papers. He discharged honorably in 1994.

After the Air Force, Chris lived at home for a while and then moved to Green Bay and Appleton, where he shared rentals with Rick, Todd, and Murf. He worked a variety of jobs during those years—as a pizza-maker and bartender, and in IT and sales. He learned computers and did network installations and support for a company part-owned by Candace. Eventually he found his niche doing phone sales for Toyota, AT&T, and TDS Metrocom. His charisma and confidence made him a natural salesperson.

Chris had a lot of fun during those carefree years of working days and spending evenings at the bar with friends. One night, Chris and Murf drove from the duplex they were renting to Fraser's, where they had a good time and several rounds of drinks. At closing time, they wisely decided to walk the few blocks home instead of driving. The next morning, Murf woke up, hungover, and saw Chris's car keys on the table. Knowing that Chris would sleep until noon, he decided to mess with him by hiding his car. He wrote a note,

"I have your car. Good luck finding me," which he wrapped around a rock and secured with rubber bands. He walked to the bar, put the rock in the parking space, and drove the car to a patch of grass behind the garage of the house, where Chris wouldn't see it when he woke up.

Later that day, after walking to the bar to get his car, Chris walked in the duplex with the rock.

"You're not gonna believe this," he told Murf, handing him the rock.

"Those bastards," Murf said. "Who would do that?"

After letting Chris stew for a few hours, Murf said, "Hey! I want to show you something." He led Chris outside to the car.

"Who the hell would park a car here?" he said.

"You bastard," Chris said, laughing and shaking his head.

Chris also loved golf, and he golfed like he lived: It was all about the fun. For a while, he and Rick worked nights at the same pizza parlor and golfed during the day at public courses because they were inexpensive. They took videos of each other and tried to improve their games, drinking and laughing their way through the course.

One summer, Chris and Rick's half-brother Jan visited Wisconsin. He was in the Air Force and was stationed in Virginia. Chris and Rick took him golfing at Midvallee Golf Course, stopping to buy beer along the way. Jan had never golfed before, and it quickly became clear that he was not a natural. He struggled through, and after the 12th hole he was feeling more confident.

The 13th hole was a long one. Jan swung and missed. On the next swing, he whiskered the, and it fell off the tee. He swung again and popped the ball in the air. Finally, he connected and drove the ball about 20 feet.

"Why don't you pick up the ball and throw it?" Chris said, laughing. Frustrated, Jan threw the ball. It hit a tree and landed behind the tee box. Chris and Rick split their sides laughing.

Rehab

Chris was moved to inpatient rehabilitation on April 10, one month and a day after his brain hemorrhaged, where he stayed another seven weeks.

Now that it was clear that Chris would survive, Holly talked to his doctors about his prognosis. Chris could move his right leg and right arm a little, but not much. More unsettling than the paralysis, though, was that Chris was unable to read and speak. Up to a point, there had been hope, however slim, that Chris would recover fully. But it became clear within a few days after he was brought out of the coma that some changes would be permanent. Which changes Chris would have to adapt to, and the extent of the changes were both unknown. Holly grieved quietly with Rich and Myra, but with Chris she showed unfailing support and encouragement.

Chris's surgeon explained that the swelling caused by the hemorrhage had put extreme pressure on Chris's brain and damaged it. It was like putting a balloon in a box, he said. When Chris's brain was bleeding, it was expanding and swelling, pressing up against the inside of his skull and taking space that simply wasn't there. The brain can handle only so much pressure, and the areas of the brain that were pressed against the skull would be damaged to some extent.

With each week, Chris recovered a little more. He began to recognize more people, including his mother, Rick, and more of his friends, including Murf, Sean, and Lisa. The tracheostomy tube was removed, and he was able to breathe through his mouth and nose again. He regained enough control over his mouth and throat to be able to eat thin foods, like soup and ice cream. His vocal cords had been paralyzed, but slowly they began to awaken. His blood pressure, which had been trending high, stabilized. His bladder function returned to normal.

Chris started physical therapy and built strength in the left side of his body, which was unaffected by the hemorrhage but very weak after weeks in the ICU. The therapist also helped him regain limited mobility and strength in his right leg and arm. Over several weeks, he gained enough strength to stand and walk with help, eventually graduating from a wheelchair to a cane by the time he was discharged.

Myra brought Christopher and Brayden back to Wisconsin in early May, and she stayed another three weeks to care for the boys. Holly and Chris hadn't seen the boys since January, and they missed them terribly. The boys missed their parents, too, especially Christopher, who was nearly four years old.

Myra took the boys to the hospital to see Chris several times each week. The first time they saw their beloved daddy, he was sitting in a wheelchair on a small, sunny porch in the hospital. Brayden, now two years old, was un-fazed by the changes in Chris, but Christopher was shy and standoffish. He was very close to Chris, and the changes in his dad made him uncomfortable.

On another visit, Chris was in bed when Myra and the boys arrived. Chris wasn't speaking words yet, but his vocal cords were recovering, and he made a noise. Christopher heard the utterance and jumped up on the bed, looking excitedly at Chris and shouting, "Brayden! Brayden! Daddy's talking! Daddy's talking!" Myra hugged Brayden, tears rolling down her cheeks.

Chris and Holly had a dog named Wah, a 120-pound black Labrador retriever. By all accounts, Wah was a great dog and loved by everyone who met him. He was well cared for by Rich, Murf, Sean, and other friends while Chris was in the hospital.

Chris loved Wah so much that his friends brought him to see Chris while he was in the rehabilitation unit. Maybe that's why *dog* was the first word Chris said when he began to speak. It was the only word he said for a while.

Everything was *dog*. If Chris wanted a glass of water, he said "dog, dog, dog, dog, dog, dog." If he had to use the bathroom, it came out as "dog, dog, dog, dog." In his mind, he was saying "I want a glass of water" and "I need to pee," but the word he spoke was *dog*. He'd look at everyone as if they were stupid because they couldn't understand that he was thirsty or needed to pee. He was unaware that he was saying "dog, dog, dog, dog."

Chris said *dog* almost exclusively while he was in rehab, but he gained a few more words, including *yes, no,* and *fish.* He also recovered the word *ham,* and he developed an unrelenting desire to sell hams door to door. In every interaction, he indicated that he no longer wanted to sit around; he wanted to sell hams. His comprehension of language spoken to him grew, too, and he began using *yes* and *no* correctly in response to simple questions.

Chris's doctors had warned Holly that Chris's personality might be extremely different when he emerged from the coma, so she was relieved that he seemed much the same person. He was delighted to see her when the doctors woke him up, and as he recovered, he was equally delighted to see his family, friends, and Wah. He also desperately wanted a cigarette and a drink.

Lisa and Sean went to the hospital nearly every day, before or after work, to support Holly and visit Chris so that she could go home to rest, eat, and take care of the house. On a sunny day in May, the nurses let Lisa and Sean take Chris for a walk in a nearby park. They bundled Chris into a wheelchair and headed out the door. He was forbidden to smoke, but he wanted nothing more than a cigarette. He couldn't say *cigarette,* but he kept miming the motions for smoking and pleading with his eyes. His friends relented, making a promise not to tell Holly, and lighted a cigarette for Chris. He was in heaven.

Home

Shortly after Chris's first embolization procedure in February, Sean and Chris were hanging out in Chris's garage, talking and drinking beer. They were listening to Stevie Ray Vaughan, which they did when they hung out. Vaughan's "Life by the Drop" was their song, and if other people thought it was funny for two dudes to have a song, these friends didn't care.

After the first embolization procedure, Chris's speech was affected a little bit, but not much. It seemed like everything would go according to plan. That evening, Sean and Chris were talking and bullshitting, laughing about the whole thing.

"What happens if I have to wear a hockey helmet and get pushed around in a wheelchair?" Chris joked.

"Stop, don't worry about it," Sean said. "Everything will be fine."

After eleven weeks in the hospital, Chris was discharged to home on May 25. He was wearing a helmet and being pushed in a wheelchair, but he was glad to be alive. He was in a helmet because the piece of skull the surgeon removed during the emergency surgery to try to stop the hemorrhage had not yet been replaced, and his brain needed to be protected.

Chris had made tremendous progress. Although he rode to the hospital exit in a wheelchair, he was able to stand, walk, and go up and down four stairs using a four-footed cane, all with minimal assistance from Holly. He could extend his right leg at the knee, and he had a trace of movement in his right ankle. His left arm and leg were getting stronger thanks to weeks of physical therapy. He still needed help with showering, bathing, and grooming, but he could dress himself with minimal assistance. He was learning new words, though he mostly said *dog*. He couldn't read, and the doctors had determined that the hemorrhage had damaged the part of Chris's brain that governs reading.

Chris had left home in March, a dreary month in Wisconsin when it seems that winter will go on forever, and he came home in full springtime, the trees fully leafed out and flowers blooming.

In preparation for his homecoming, Rich and Nat, Holly's brother, had built handrails on the stairs leading to the front and back doors of the duplex and installed grab bars in other spots where Chris might need them. Nat helped Chris get home from the hospital and into the duplex. He was home, and he began adjusting to his new life.

Myra stayed in Wisconsin until the last week of May to help Chris, Holly, and the boys transition to being together again. She wanted to make their lives seem as normal as possible, and she worked on helping the boys and Chris reestablish the strong bond they'd had before the hemorrhage.

The boys were very young and had tons of energy and questions, but Chris was still recovering. He slept a lot, watched TV, and was wrapped in a blanket because he was always cold. When he tried to speak to them, he lost his patience easily because he couldn't say what was in his head. Even when he could say what he wanted, Chris had little control over the volume of his voice, and what he said often came out loud and harsh, as if he were barking orders at the boys.

At first, Holly and Myra intervened because the boys got scared, but gradually they backed off. Myra encouraged the boys to learn to interpret Chris's responses, and Holly recognized that she had to help them understand Chris's limitations. "Daddy doesn't mean to yell at you," she said as the boys got used to Chris's new voice. "He loves you very much."

Holly had taken a leave of absence from work, and she managed the details of Chris's condition with determination. She asked as many questions as she needed to understand what had to be done to maximize his recovery. She helped Chris adapt and learn, encouraged him, and managed the many therapy and follow-up appointments with Chris's medical team. She also took on the many tasks of running the household, parenting the boys, and dealing with the frustrating details of insurance. There was a lot for the family to adjust to.

Chris received therapy at home for several weeks before transitioning to appointments out of the house. He had physical therapy to improve his overall strength and coordination, occupational therapy to regain function in his right arm and hand, and speech therapy to work on comprehending and producing language.

A month after his discharge, Chris returned to Theda Clark Hospital for surgery to have the piece of his skull that was removed during the emergency surgery in March replaced. He walked using a cane that day, with help from Holly. Prior to the procedure, he and Holly communicated to the doctors that he'd had headaches and dizziness since returning home. He indicated that he felt his speech was improving, but that he still had a long way to go. Holly said she felt that his language skills were stable.

The surgery to replace the bone went smoothly. In addition, the PEG feeding tube in his stomach was removed, moving Chris another step closer to normalcy.

By early July, Chris's language was indeed improving. He was seen by his doctor for a follow-up appointment, who noted that Chris was able to say *Holly* easily. He was also able to repeat a word spoken to him. He still had trouble saying his own name, and he was working on saying the boys' names. He had begun trying to focus on thinking about what he wanted to say instead letting *dog* come out as the expression of his thought. His comprehension was improving, too, and he was able to follow most of the doctor's one-word instructions. Physically, Chris was able to shrug his right shoulder, bend his right elbow and wrist slightly, and flex the fingers of his right hand a bit. He had movement in his right knee, but not in his ankle. He was gaining more control over his right side generally. He was making slow, steady progress.

When Chris saw one of his doctors a month later, he showed more improvement. He was walking with a standard, single-point cane instead of a four-footed cane. He could say more words, including *yes,* but he still had difficulty saying *no,* and he relied heavily on hand gestures to make his wants and needs known. He could say *Christopher* and *Brayden,* an accomplishment that made him very happy. The doctor noted that he was recovering with aggressive therapy, rehab, and a very supportive wife.

Holly returned to work in August after a five-month leave of absence. Family and friends stepped up to help with the transition.

Myra flew back from Alabama to stay with the family for three weeks. She took over driving Chris to therapy appointments, taking the boys to daycare, and keeping the household going while everyone adjusted to Holly being away from the house during the day.

Practical and no-nonsense, Myra focused on helping Chris recover to the point that he could take care of himself while Holly was at work. Chris was a very good cook, and he had done most of the cooking after he and Holly got married. He took special pride in his ribs, an all-day event that started with a dry rub followed by roasting them in the oven, smothering them in barbeque sauce and transferring them to the grill for a long, slow cook over low heat. Myra set about teaching Chris to cook one-handed, starting with a fried egg sandwich using a Little Mac hamburger cooker she had bought for Holly when she was in college. Once he had mastered the sandwich, she worked with him on other meals he could make with one hand.

When she left, she took Christopher and Brayden back home with her to Alabama for several weeks to let Chris and Holly get back into their new routine.

Rick took over driving Chris to therapy appointments when Myra went back to Alabama. He was doing freelance work at the time, and he had time during the day.

Rick also tried some therapy of his own with Chris. He had read about a brain scientist who'd had a brain hemorrhage and documented her experience and recovery. She had been successful in using a mirror to show her nonfunctional hand in the position of her functional hand and trick her brain into believing that the nonfunctional hand was, in fact, the functional hand. The trick spurred her brain to develop new neural pathways, and the nonfunctional hand recovered. Rick and Chris tried the technique for about five months, but it didn't work for Chris.

Chris's friends were loyal and helpful, too. Rich continued to help with Wah and other tasks around the duplex. Others visited him frequently. Sean was working third shift, and he visited Chris a few times a week before he went to work. He brought over McDonald's and they'd watch cooking shows like Bobby Flay and Guy Fieri while they ate their burgers.

They gathered for campfires at Sean's house, just as they had before the hemorrhage. Their first campfire was special, though, because everyone—Rich, Murf, Sean, Lisa, Holly, and Chris, who was wrapped in blanket—was wearing a shirt printed with "Dawg Dawg" on the front. Chris's friends had written funny stories about Chris, which they called the Book of Questions. They played the Book of Questions as a game, posing one question after another. One question was "If there was one word you could remove from your vocabulary, what would it be?"

"Dog!" Chris answered. Everyone burst into laughter. His sense of humor had survived.

A test done on Chris's brain at the end of July showed that blood continued to flow through the AVM. Although it was smaller, the AVM measured approximately three centimeters in diameter, a reduction of one-and-a-half centimeters from when it was first measured. Despite all he had been through, Chris was still at risk for another hemorrhage. A third embolization procedure or additional surgery were far too risky. CyberKnife stereotactic radiosurgery was the only option left, and it was the best chance for obliterating the remaining AVM.

Stereotactic radiosurgery uses precise, highly intense doses of radiation to destroy tumors and lesions. It is similar in accuracy to a surgeon's scalpel, hence the name

CyberKnife. In Chris's case, the radiation would damage and cause scarring in the veins and arteries of the AVM, which would then form blood clots and shrivel over several years.

Chris had the CyberKnife procedure on September 9. Although the procedure went smoothly, it would take several years to determine whether the AVM would be eliminated completely. At a follow-up appointment, the doctor informed him that he was still at risk for seizures and another hemorrhage, and he recommended that Chris continue taking Keppra, the anti-seizure medication that was prescribed to him in December.

Chris continued physical therapy and speech therapy throughout the rest of the year. He was frustrated with progress that he saw as slow, but his speech therapist was encouraging. She reported that he was able to say more single words while pointing to objects, and he was beginning to speak in short phrases. He was working with an iPad, which was helping him increase his vocabulary. His physical therapist encouraged him to do more stretching and exercises at home to increase his walking speed and avoid losing strength in his right leg.

Chris got his driver's license renewed in 2008, an accomplishment that gave him great satisfaction. His license had expired while he was in the hospital, and he wanted to resume driving as soon as he could. He had to start at the beginning, learning to drive with his left arm and leg, taking the vision test, and passing the written test.

Sean taught Chris how to drive again, riding with him for safety as he was starting out. In preparation, he helped get Chris's vehicle adapted so that he could operate the gas and brake pedals with his left foot. As Chris drove, Sean watched for other cars, too, to help Chris adapt to the loss of some peripheral vision in his right eye. His vision improved as he recovered and allowed him to pass the vision test.

Rick helped Chris study for the written test, and he drove him to the DMV to take the test. Chris took the test orally, using headphones because he couldn't read the questions. He took it five times before he passed. When Holly was comfortable with Chris driving the boys, he began driving them to daycare and picking them up.

Dammit

Dammit was one word that returned fairly quickly to Chris's vocabulary. *Dammit* came easily when other words wouldn't, and through it Chris expressed his frustration with his new limitations. Chris was fiercely independent and wanted to speak and do things for himself, but even the smallest tasks were a challenge, from putting on socks, brushing his teeth, and finding the words to express his thoughts. Chris worked at every challenge to the point of extreme frustration, and his frustration fueled his recovery. In fact, at one point in his recovery Holly wondered whether Chris was depressed because he was becoming less frustrated.

Murf made it his mission to teach Chris sentences. He and Chris made up guy-talk sentences, and the two went to the bar to work on them. Chris was happy to get back to bar life. Rick had taken him on his first outing to a bar in a wheelchair, where Chris had his first post-hemorrhage drink. "Wow! Drunk!" he'd said.

Every time Murf and Chris went to the bar, they worked on one new sentence. Murf proposed sentences for polite company and for guys-at-the-bar company, which were less polite but that made them laugh. They kept a running list that Chris kept folded in his wallet.

The polite-company sentences Murf and Chris wrote together were clean:

"It is nice out today."

"You get what you pay for."

Of course, there were sentences about the Packers:

"The Packers kick ass!"

"First down!"

"Punt him in the giblets!" (The perfect sentence when the Packers were having a hard time.)

The less polite sentences made them laugh:

"Me, hemorrhage. What the fuck's wrong with you?"

"Hi! My name's Chris. You're a hottie!"

"That's a big fucking burger!"

There were a few aimed directly at Murf:

"You're an asshole!"

"Here's to you, and here's to me, best of friends we will always be. If we should ever disagree, fuck you, and here's to me."

But the one sentence that sized up Chris's new life situation was the one he learned first. Murf had taken Chris to the bar one night, and they had worked on the sentence. The next evening Chris, Holly, Murf, and friends went to Sean's for a campfire in the back yard. They were drinking beer and talking, and Murf said, "Hey, Chris! Say your sentence!"

Chris stood up, steadied himself, and said, "Fuck you and the horse you rode in on!"

Shocked but laughing, Holly said, "Murf! My husband hasn't said a decent sentence in months, and that's the first thing he says?!" But she understood it for what it was—the perfect metaphor for all Chris had been through.

After several months, Chris could say most of the sentences, but some nights at the bar were harder than others. One evening, Chris had been unable to say the sentence they'd worked on and was frustrated. To add to that, as they were driving home, Chris was trying to tell Murf something, but he couldn't get enough of it out for Murf to get the gist. They worked on it as they drove, Murf asking questions and Chris getting increasingly frustrated. He gave up, and a few moments later came out with "I'll think about it tomorrow." He'd said his sentence. The two friends cheered.

Chris's unofficial therapy continued as life settled into a new rhythm. His speech improved dramatically by talking to his family and friends, and he made peace with the paralysis in his right arm and leg. But he wanted to communicate more effectively, and he wanted to work on reading. He and Holly made an appointment to see his doctor in 2011, who agreed with Chris's request for a new round of speech therapy.

Chris made some significant strides during eight weeks of therapy. He added words to his vocabulary and improved his speaking fluency. His comprehension of spoken language improved. He made progress toward reading fundamentals, too, matching letters to their sounds 87 percent of the time, compared to 15 percent of the time when he started, but he remained unable to read full words. Unfortunately, the therapy ended when Chris's insurance benefits for the calendar year were used up despite his demonstrated progress toward several goals.

The progress Chris made during therapy led the speech therapist to give him a diagnosis of moderate Broca's aphasia at the conclusion of the eight weeks, an adjustment of his original diagnosis of severe Broca's aphasia in 2007.

Broadly defined, aphasia is an impairment of language, which can include speaking, understanding, reading, and writing. Aphasia is always due to an injury to the brain, such as a stroke, head injury, brain tumor, or in Chris's case, a hemorrhage from a ruptured AVM. Aphasia varies tremendously from person to person: For some, language can be relatively unaffected; others can have extreme difficulty communicating. For Chris, all four areas of language were affected.

Broca's aphasia is a type of aphasia that results from an injury to speech and language areas of the brain, such as the left hemisphere, which is where Chris's AVM was located. People with Broca's aphasia often have trouble coming up with words and producing grammatical sentences, and some have more difficulty using verbs than nouns. Chris's speech fit this diagnosis. He had a hard time saying the words that were in his head, his sentences were mostly short and ungrammatical, and he relied heavily on nouns. Interestingly, some people with Broca's aphasia sing well.

Others are very adept a swearing. Chris didn't sing much, but he could swear, which helped him vent his frustration.

Damage to the Broca's area of the brain can also affect a person's ability to comprehend spoken language. Depending on the damage, a person may understand speech relatively well, particularly when the grammar is simple, and the content is somewhat familiar and expected. For instance, a person diagnosed with Broca's aphasia might easily understand the sentence "Nathan drove John to school" and struggle with "John was driven to school by Nathan" because Nathan, the driver, appears at the end of the sentence. Understanding the relationship requires an understanding of sentence grammar, which comes naturally to an undamaged brain. Chris was able to comprehend straightforward sentences like "Nathan drove John to school," and his language comprehension improved during therapy. However, he was unable meet the goal of understanding a full paragraph of new information.

Chris continued to work on learning to read on his own, using his iPad to match pictures and words read aloud with written words. He retained some residual reading capacity. For example, he correctly identified the words *park, cow, musician,* and *lamp* when presented in a group of four words on his iPad. When shown a book with *little* in the title, he asked if the word was *baby.*

Chris's ability to read, write, and express numbers was less affected than his ability to read and write words. For example, in response to a question about when he and Holly got married, he could write *2002*, and he used digits to say the year, saying "two zero zero two" rather than "two thousand two." Similarly, when asked to read *2002*, he correctly said "two zero zero two." To express smaller numbers, he needed to count up. If he planned to meet someone at a restaurant at 7:00 PM, for instance, he would say "Meet at one, two three, four, five, six, seven. Seven."

Chris's ability to read numbers helped tremendously as he relearned how to drive. He was able to interpret speed limit signs and adjust his speed accordingly, even though he expressed speed limits in digits: "three zero" for *thirty* and "four five" for *forty-five*. Also useful for driving was his retained ability to recognize red and green, even though he didn't associate the colors with the words *red* and *green*. "That one means go," he said at a traffic light.

Chris's spatial sense was also seemingly unaffected. He learned to use Google Maps to find a destination and follow the app's verbal instructions. He also learned to use the app effectively in conversations about places. For example, when asked about where he was deployed in the Air Force, he was unable to come up with the name of the country. He used Google Maps to find the answer: He pinched the screen to get to the world map, swiped to move the map to the Middle East, and enlarged it again to point to Saudi Arabia. When asked, "Were you in Saudi Arabia?" he said, "Yes! Saudi Arabia. Air Force. Desert Storm." Similarly, when asked which hospital he was in during 2007, he was unable to say the name *Theda Clark Hospital,* but he navigated to it easily on his phone.

The words Chris spoke remained easy to understand. Although his right arm and leg were paralyzed, the muscles on the right side of his face were unaffected. Chris's speech was clear and loud; his challenge was coming up with enough words for the listener to grasp his thought. With an actively engaged conversationalist, he could usually make himself understood; with someone who refused to try, it was much harder.

One evening, Chris and Sean were having a few drinks around a campfire with their friend Jeffrey Schmedlin, whom they called Schmed. The three guys were talking about what music to listen to. Chris kept saying, "little pig, little pig," but Sean and Schmed didn't know what he was talking about. Chris tried to come up with more information, but he couldn't. He kept trying. "Dammit! Little pig, little pig!" he said. After nearly an hour, it clicked for Sean: Chris wanted to listen to "Three Little Pigs" by the band Green Jelly. The three friends toasted their moment of triumph.

New Normal

Chris and his family settled into their new normal.

Chris tried to return to work several times, taking jobs at Goodwill and in a bar, but he found more fulfillment as a stay-at-home dad in the new house he and Holly bought in a quiet subdivision. He took on many responsibilities involved in having a family: getting the boys ready for school, driving them to and from school and activities, cooking for the family, and taking care of Wah and Hunter, the dog the family got when Wah died. He also handled many household chores, like grocery shopping, laundry, and yardwork. Holly moved into human resources, and she earned enough to support the family.

Like little speech therapists, Christopher and Brayden talked all the time, helping Chris learn new words and say them more easily. In fact, Chris and Holly noticed that his speech declined when the boys visited Myra over the summer.

Chris continued to work on speech and reading with his iPad, and he learned to send simple texts using the speech-recognition feature on his phone. Physically, he got stronger by working with a trainer at the YMCA during the day. As the boys grew up, he worked out while Christopher took martial arts classes after school and in the evenings. Although he continued to walk with a limp, he rarely used his cane, keeping it in his vehicle in case he needed it.

Chris maintained his connection with his friends. He and Holly stood up at Sean and Lisa's wedding. He found a new local bar, Dieter's, where he went on Wednesdays to catch up with the crowd. On Fridays he met Murf at the Lake Park for fish fry, and he met Rich at the bar to watch the Packers. He resumed playing poker every two months with his friends—Rich, Sean, Murf, Schmed, and a few neighbors—who rotated among houses to play cards, drink, smoke, and talk. Chris remained close to Todd's sister, Terri, and he spent Thanksgiving with Todd's family each year.

Chris's new normal was threatened In October of 2014, more than seven years after the hemorrhage, when he began feeling ill and having headaches. He went to his primary care doctor, who prescribed antibiotics and advised him to treat his symptoms with Tylenol, adequate fluids, and rest. He told Chris to call if his symptoms persisted or worsened.

Several days later, Holly brought Chris to the emergency room. He'd had a headache for ten days, and at this point it was constant and severe. He had vomited all night and into the morning. He was having some trouble understanding simple requests, like "touch your nose." The ER doctor ordered blood tests and a CT scan of Chris's head. The blood tests showed that Chris's white blood cell count was elevated, suggesting an infection. His platelets were also elevated. The CT scan was compared to the scan done in 2008, revealing a collection of fluid larger and denser than was present in 2008. A second CT scan, done with contrast fluid, confirmed the presence of fluid. The ER doctor feared that Chris was having another hemorrhage and admitted him to the hospital. Soon after he was transferred by ambulance to Theda Clark Hospital, where his initial surgery was done.

At the hospital, he was started on intravenous antibiotics in case the problem was an infection, not a hemorrhage, since his white blood cell count was well above normal. (The oral antibiotics prescribed by Chris's primary care physician weren't in his notes, and Chris hadn't started taking them.) He had a four-vessel cerebral angiogram and two MRIs, with contrast and without, to check the status of the AVM. Each test revealed a slowly expanding collection of fluid. The doctors suspected a new, slow hemorrhage, and they proposed surgery to clear out the fluid. Chris and Holly agreed.

The surgery took place on October 27. Happily, the surgeon found only residual evidence of the AVM, which meant that the CyberKnife radiosurgery procedure done in 2007 had been successful. However, the fluid collecting in Chris's brain was perhaps more dangerous than a hemorrhage might have been: It was a rare staph infection in the cotton balls the surgeon had placed in Chris's brain during the emergency surgery in 2007 to stop the uncontrolled bleeding. The surgeon cleaned out as much fluid as he could, closed up Chris's brain, and ordered eight weeks of intravenous vancomycin, one of the strongest antibiotics available. Chris went home on Halloween, four days after the surgery.

Myra came and stayed for several weeks to help Chris so that Holly could go back to work, starting up Chris's antibiotics every eight hours through a port in his chest. She had never done anything like that before, and she worried that she might harm Chris. She told her husband, "I am scared to death, but I can't let Holly know because she's got too much on her mind. She has to feel confident I can do this." She was relieved when home care provided a pump.

Chris felt better within a week, and—somewhat miraculously—he recovered fully.

Afterword

Fast forward eleven years from 2007. In the summer of 2018, I took a drive with Chris. He drove remarkably well, even with no use of his right arm or leg. He was impatient with slow drivers and a little late on the brake for my liking, but he drove safely.

He wanted to show me where he grew up. He used Google Maps to navigate from Appleton to Oconto County, but once we crossed into his home territory, he pulled off the road at a quiet spot and closed the app.

"GPS all done," Chris said. "I'm home."

From there, he drove easily from Gillett to Underhill to Bonduel, where he finished high school, stopping at points in between: the two houses he lived in as a child, the park where he went sledding in the winter, Rich's childhood home, Terri's store, the spot where he had a car wreck as a teenager late on a weekend night ("Little bit drunk," he said). A tractor had pulled his car out of the ditch.

We were circling a bit in Underhill as Chris pointed out the house he lived in and the park on the Oconto River he played in. A curious neighbor spotted the car and came out her house to ask if we needed directions. Together, Chris and I explained who he was. The neighbor, in her seventies, remembered his family. Her daughter, who drove up a few minutes later, had babysat Chris and Rick.

The more Chris talked about things he knew and remembered, the more fluent his speech became. As he connected with people interested in him and willing to understand him, the more he relaxed into the charismatic person he still is.

Later that summer, I spent the afternoon with Chris, Christopher, and Brayden. The boys were now teenagers: Christopher was heading into his sophomore year of high school, and Brayden was entering eighth grade. They had just returned from their summer visit to Myra, where they had spent a month or six weeks every summer since they were babies. As they grew up, she came to Wisconsin during their last week of school to go on their end-of-school field trips, and then the three of them flew to Alabama until mid-July. They were fortunate to have caring grandparents. The summer before, Candace had taken the boys and Chris on a road trip, spending two weeks exploring Yellowstone, Mt. Rushmore, Crazy Horse, and the Badlands. Before Mike's death in 2016, Candace had rented a cottage each summer, spending a week swimming and having bonfires on the shores of Shawano Lake.

Like their dad, the boys were outgoing, funny, and talkative. Both talked about themselves: Christopher was into computers, gaming, and martial arts, and Brayden was more into music. Christopher was learning how to cook, and Chris gave him instructions on how to finish the beef stew he had started earlier. Brayden interjected funny, gentle jabs at his brother and Chris, and talked more seriously about his ambition to be a pilot as he explained the physics of flight.

There was a lot of interaction, interruption, laughter, and good-natured teasing when they talked together about their communication with each other. It's no wonder Chris learned to talk as well as he did.

Christopher remembered Chris giving them one-word commands as children, "like he would give the dog," he said. He knew what Chris meant then, but conversation became much more normal as Chris learned more phrases. "I usually get the gist of what he's saying, and then I figure out the details," he said. "He gives pretty good clues. I understand 99.99 percent of what he's trying to say."

Chris is "just Dad," Brayden said. They figure things out, sometimes getting frustrated and impatient, but with love and humor. Brayden put it this way: "Sometimes he gets frustrated and then we [referring to Christopher and himself] get frustrated and then it's like, none of us can talk to each other at all. We go to our 30-minute corners for a break. Then we come back, Dad says the exact same thing, and we say 'Oh! I get it now! How did I not get that?'"

There's a lot of give and take, according to Brayden. "We kind of have to be translators for each other, in a way," he said. "He'll say something, and we either interpret it the same way or a different way, and he has to let us know if that's what he means. It's like a code."

While Chris is "just Dad" to his sons, to his friends he has become an example of perseverance. More than once during the interviews Chris and I conducted, people who know him best commented that the hemorrhage has brought out the strength of his character and personality. They recognized that for someone as outspoken, dynamic, and full of life as Chris to lose his ability to read, write, and express himself was—and continues to be—incredibly difficult. But they stressed that he has adapted to a situation no one wants or asks for. He learned to deal with his paralysis and now walks, drives, and cooks. He expanded his vocabulary from *dog* to many words as well as phrases and sentences, and he works incredibly hard to express himself even when the words in his head just won't come.

Chris's friend Sean said, "If Chris can handle life, I can stop whining," acknowledging the challenges Chris meets head on day after day. Indeed, when we consider what many of us do every day with ease through the lens of Chris's post-hemorrhage life—whether it's walking into a restaurant, writing a grocery list, explaining an idea, reading this book, or the hundreds of actions we do without noticing or appreciating—Chris's triumph over injury and adversity has been nothing short of amazing. He meets challenges large and small every day, conquering them one at a time.